Famous Fleets
Series
Volume Nine

Great Western
Railway
Road Vehicles
Part II

Alan Earnshaw

Nostalgia Road Publications

CONTENTS

The **Nostalgia Road - Famous Fleets** Series™

is designed and published by

Trans-Pennine Publishing Ltd.
PO Box 10,
Appleby-in-Westmorland,
Cumbria, CA16 6FA
Tel.+44 (0)17683 51053 Fax.+44 (0)17683 53558

trade enquiries: www.nostalgiaroad.co.uk
personal shoppers: www.transpenninepublishing.co.uk

and printed by
Kent Valley Colour Printers Ltd.
Kendal, Cumbria +44 (0)1539 741344

© Text: Trans-Pennine Publishing Ltd. 2008-9
© Photographs: Great Western Railway or
British Railways (WR) or as credited.

Cover & Title Page: *A stunning and delightful image of rural life in the mid-1930s is pictured by this Thornycroft Handy 2-ton drop-side and trailer employed on the Country Lorry Service near Lechlade.*

Rear Cover Top: *The way it used to be - horse and cartage operations depicted at Steam in Swindon, which is well worth visiting.* **Alan Earnshaw**

Rear Cover Bottom: *No we haven't lost our wits, this is a surviving GWR Foden that the Manchester firm of George Sanders bought, direct from British Railways, for £250 in 1962; it is still in their fleet today.* **Alan Earnshaw**

This Page: *The GWR road motor fleet is perhaps best known for its work on milk collection and delivery, as seen here at Lostwithiel.*

INTRODUCTION

When Bill Aldridge and I began writing our books on railway-owned road vehicles, we never imagined how successful and widely regarded the subject would become. It spurred on the Railways & Roads event at the National Railway Museum in York, from where our good friend Bob Gwynne encouraged other preserved railway groups to take on the organisation of similar events around the country.

Today such events have become hugely popular with road and railway enthusiasts alike, and each has now got a better understanding of the other side's perspective on things. Yet it can be rightly said that the development of road transport owes much to the railway companies in the 'Big Four' era, who themselves were once the world's largest road fleet operators.

Above: *The second of three views showing the Nestlé Creamery at Lostwithiel in Cornwall during October 1932. This important agricultural community began supplying milk to London (as well as Bristol and the West Midlands) in 1932, although it had been connected to Plymouth and Bristol by railway in 1859. The line made it much easier for tourists to reach Cornwall, and railway workshops were subsequently built in the town. In 1869 a branch railway opened to the picturesque port of Fowey, and thereafter Lostwithiel remained an important junction until the branch closed to all traffic in January 1965. The series of views from which this taken were obviously publicity images, but it serves to show that the road vehicle fleet employed not only different types of chassis and body, but different colour schemes as well; note the two-deck churn-carrying body on the new Morris five-ton lorry.*

It is some eight years since we published *GWR Road Vehicles*, but it still remains a popular title and thus indicates the demand for more knowledge on the subject. Ironically, it was whilst meeting with the two authors of a forthcoming book (*British Rail Vehicles 1969-1990*) Gerald Burton and Bill Gable, that Bill diffidently pulled out a packet of old GWR pictures and said "are these any use".

The images were all prints from full-plate glass negatives, and although crumbling round the edges, they provided some superb detail that could not be seen in the pictures used in our original GWR book. For railway and road modellers, this detail is an absolute god-send, and we therefore make no excuse in using the images as big as we can in this volume, whilst referring our readers to the earlier edition (or what we now call *GWR Road Vehicles Part I*) for a full textual reference.

Below: *The third of the Lostwithiel pictures shows five of the ten vehicles the GWR had allocated there. These included, from left to right, No.1905 a four-ton Associated Daimler model 508, No.2461 a re-built Maudslay Express Cartage van (which was given one of the Swindon-made GWR radiators), No.2905 a six-ton Morris Commercial up-rated at Swindon to four-tons and a Thornycroft with drop-sides, and a pair of two-ton Thornycroft Handy drop-sides (registered consecutively as GX 3258 and 3259), Nod.3258/9. Also in the Lostwithiel fleet were the three new five-ton Morris trucks Nos.2902-4 (see* GWR Road Vehicles Vol. 1 *page 36 top right for a close up view of these trucks), and another pair of Associated Daimler model 508s, Nos.2459 and 2460. All three Associated Daimlers had been converted from Express Cartage box vans of the kind pictured on page 22 top right of Part One.*

EXPRESS CARTAGE VEHICLES

As already outlined in Part One, this was the most prestigious part of the GWR's road vehicle operation, and it was where they used their best vehicles. What was not apparent at the time of our writing the original book was the fact that the majority of vehicles employed on the Express service were no more than three-years-old, as the GWR then had a policy of cascading their vehicles down to lesser important services as they progressively aged. When you study the photographs in this book very closely, you can see how true this is, but I must record my thanks to James Steadman, whose father was a GWR driver, for writing and pointing this out to me.

Above: *Not only did the GWR cascade its Express Cartage Service vehicles down to lesser duties on a regular basis, but they also painted them on an annual basis. Here we see a 1926 Thornycroft two-ton van (YN 231), which became No.950 in the fleet. The Swindon Works body is notable, as it has a distinct look of railway rolling stock building about it. The driver has the benefit of a padded leather seat, with room for a 'mate' alongside, plus access into the van body from the cab. However, it will be obvious to all that his was not a comfortable job, as only a shallow scuttle and overhanging roof were provided to keep out the elements. The solid tyres would not be much fun when driving along the cobbled or unmade streets of the era.*

Above: *Slightly more comfortable, this later Thornycroft model (No.2015 in the GWR fleet) still has a Swindon-built body, but the cab has the benefit of a windscreen and half-doors. It also has gone to a forward-control layout and has been provided with pneumatic tyres. The view dates from October 1930 when the vehicle was given electric headlights to work alongside its acetylene lamps.*

Left: *Whilst the vehicles of the Road Motor Department may not have had the height of luxury that drivers' cabs have today, they were certainly a vast improvement on the open drays and 'lurries' used by the horse-drawn vehicles. In this un-dated view, two of Exeter Depot's horse teams have put their dray and tilt van on display at a local show.*

Above: *Having had a successful period of operating the Morris Commercial 'T-Type' van (after its introduction in 1924), the GWR continued to purchase further examples of the Marque in the years ahead. This 'C-Type' No.2583 (GX 2923) was one of a batch of 30 two-ton models delivered to Swindon Works as chassis-cowl models in July and August 1932. This example, later No.2245, was turned out as a normal-control model and allocated to the Railhead Delivery Service. Note the large advertising panel behind the cab doors.*

Right: *This rear view of No.2583 will be of special interest to modellers, as it shows in some detail the interior of the van body. Note the boxes over the wheel arches, the slatted upper sides (to allow loads to be tied down) and the moveable ladder that gave access to the roof rack.*

Top Left: *Not all the Morris Commercial 'C-Type' chassis acquired in the summer of 1932 were fitted with normal control bodies, as both semi-forward-control and full forward-control versions were produced. According to the GWR records, there were no semi-forward-control models at all, although this image shows otherwise. Even the pencilled legend on the back refers to it as a two-ton forward-control model. Yet, the author has seen several pictures which, although they are too poor to reproduce in this book, clearly show 'C-Type' vehicles with the flat front that was required for a true forward-control vehicle. It is interesting to note that several vehicles in this batch had a demountable body, in this case No.2004. The vehicle was later fitted with a permanent body and re-numbered as No.2361 in the GWR fleet. However, this is not included in the fleet lists shown later, as it is understood that it never carried that number in revenue-earning service.*

Bottom Left: *By the end of the 1930s, the GWR were starting to acquire lighter vans for the Express Cartage Service, mostly in the 25- to 30-cwt range. This was not because the loads were decreasing, but because the reliability of vehicle chassis was improving. Additional to this was the fact that the Government were willing to part-fund vehicles in this weight range, as they could later be used for military or civil defence purposes in the war that was obviously looming in Europe. A classic example of this policy is found with this 'Joint Express Service' vehicle that was operated in conjunction with the LMS. Forerunners of the inter-station parcel vans (symbolised by their black and white chequered bands in BR days), vans like this 30-cwt Morris Commercial ran between Paddington Station and the London terminals of the LMS. They were mostly used to transfer advance luggage and parcels between these great termini, fulfiling a vital service for the travelling public. This image was taken at Swindon Works on 28th January 1939, but the vehicle was later used as an ARP ambulance.*

GENERAL SERVICE VEHICLES

In Part One, we discussed in detail the evolution of the GWR Road Motor Department, but this did not only provide revenue-earning vehicles, but at the time also supplied them for the service departments of the railway company. For instance the Civil Engineers, Railway Workshops, Signalling & Telegraph and Shipping departments all had their own sub-fleets within the Road Motor Department.

Ostensibly, these may have looked to be separate entities, but recent records show that the road fleet was considered as a whole, and not just a sum of parts. This is of course very important to remember, especially when the practice of cascading older vehicles was being implemented.

Above: *This Thornycroft PB 30-cwt lorry was new to the cartage fleet at Paddington as No.947 in March 1926. Note the hoops for the canvas tilt and the way they fit the flat bed.*

Quite naturally, the manager of Cartage Department or an S&T depot, did not want somebody-else's cast offs, especially if the bodywork was battered or scruffy. The policy of having demountable bodies, which could be swapped and repaired, helped to combat this problem, but it is also evident that the other departments were allowed a certain percentage of new vehicles and did not have to rely on hand-me-downs from the Express Cartage Services Department. This was especially important for those departments needing vehicles with a heavier payload than those normally used on express parcels work.

Left: *The idea of the demountable body almost certainly originated in the Engineer's Department at Paddington during the early 1920s, but it would take many years for the practice to become an industry-standard. Similarly the idea of a curtain-side is a GWR innovation, and in the picture to the left we can see one of the early examples of this on the 1904 horse-drawn three-ton wagon No.2648. Whilst this is only the hoop and canvas tilt concept, it is easy to see where modern vehicle designers got their inspiration. But how about the body on the two-ton Thornycroft PB in the foreground? The load-carrying body featured on No.1334 is a novel idea of combining a fixed van body and a sliding tilt. By pushing the moveable portion of the body back over the fixed part, the rear end of the lorry can be left open to the elements. In such a way it can carry larger or taller than normal loads, such as the 'packing case' containing push cycle wheels and frames. This image was taken in West London on 27th July 1927. Again the lorry still has solid rubber wheels.*

Top Right: *The first book on this subject showed a number of photographs of AEC Y-Type lorries, including one on page 26. This was a 3¹/2-ton open-cabbed model converted for use with a demountable body system. We subsequently discovered the view was taken at Paddington on a rainy 25th June 1925. Also on the same date a four- to five-ton Y-Type was being tested with the Rendell Demountable Loading System. This vehicle AC 94 had a strengthened chassis and a heavier back axle, but was still cursed with a 'pram hood' over the driving position, This view shows the demountable bed and how the cab was 'offset', allowing the driver more visibility to look over his shoulder to check on his load. Careful observation will reveal, on the left of the truck, the 'exhausting fumes' left behind by other members in the cartage fleet at Paddington!*

Bottom Right: *Demountable bodies were not always needed in the GWR fleet, and this smart little Ford A-Type truck for the Hotels Department demonstrates that not all of the GWR's road vehicle fleet were painted in the brown and cream that is almost universally applied by railway modellers who have period vehicles on their layouts. This vehicle was finished in very dark brown colour scheme, not the more common chocolate, and had writing GWR in cream. However, it is important to note that the font style used in all three instances (on the cab, the canvas tilt and the lorry side) is completely different to one another! The fleet number plate 1022 would have been black lettering on a white background.*

11

Above: *I have to be fairly honest and say that I really do not know much about the GWR's road steamers and in Part One my co-author commented that by 1909 the fleet numbered just three such vehicles. After this a letter was received from John L. Watson of Exmouth stating that his father had driven a four-wheeled coal lorry S18 [sic] in the Exeter area during the 1920s. It was therefore quite fascinating to find this lovely picture of S-18 at Exeter in December 1929.*

It is of course a Foden steam lorry, but slightly less common than the normal examples, in its having a twin rear axle. The drop-sides have been fitted with extension boards, and in this case UL 4362 is carrying a full load of bales of straw (in GWR sacks). The builder's plate on the side reads 'Royal Letters Patent 13296. Fodens Limited Sandbach, England'. It was ten-tons unladen weight and could carry a weight of four-tons. The legend on the rear hub caps states 'Foden Six-Wheeler'.

Above: *The arrival of the standard railway container in 1929 was covered on page 25 of part one of this story. However, in these two photographs we have a pair of excellent views of the press and publicity demonstration held at Paddington Goods Yard in December 1929 using a four-ton container (B-88) and Thornycroft two-ton lorry No.1336 (YE 5402) The first image clearly shows the container being loaded using a portable yard crane. Container B-105 is seen on flat wagon 11493 behind, whilst B-82 is on a horse-drawn dray to the right of the model PB lorry.*

Right: *The same lorry and container, this time being handled by a six-ton yard crane at Paddington. Note the excellent rear view of the container with its drop-down tailgate on fold-back upper doors.*

Above: *In the early days of the GWR's Road Motor Department, the AEC Y-Type was an important member of the fleet, especially after a large number of ex-War Department AECs were acquired from 1919 onwards. Fitted with interchangeable bodies, these remained a big part of the front-line service for a decade or more. Here we see No.1928 a four- to five-ton chassis fitted with flat-bed body G1016 at Paddington on 15th March 1929.*

Left: *The Thornycroft PB was another key member of the fleet during the 1920s, as we see here with No.1334 pictured at the maker's works in Basingstoke. The image is well worth inclusion as it shows the extent to which the sliding cargo canopy could be drawn forward, although it is very doubtful whether it would ever be driven like this.*

Above: *The Thornycroft PB was used in many guises by the GWR, ranging from forward-control Express Cartage delivery vans to buses, six-wheel drop-side trucks used by both the sundries fleet and various engineering departments. Another example of the PB in non-revenue-earning service is found with fleet number 2249 (GK 6149), which is seen here with*

tipper body G.1949. This was described as an 'ash, cinder or ballast tipper', and the capacity measured by cubic yards and not the more common tons. The manual stated that the body 'will carry five cu.yds. of ballast or six cu.yds. of ash or cinders.' Small cast-iron plates at either end of the tipper body show the height levels of the respective capacities.

Above: *From the dairy collection vehicle and the country lorry service pictures shown earlier, it will be appreciated that a lot of the GWR's rural traffic was connected with the farming community. In the days when many animals were still walked to the market for sale, the railways provided a much more suitable alternative. Obviously, when a farmer fattened up an animal for slaughter, it was counterproductive to then walk it 50 or 100 miles to market! Obviously a walked animal would subsequently lose weight and may need fattening up again when it reached the city where it was to be slaughtered, which was often a costly affair. The railways were therefore a god-send for the livestock farmers, as they could get their beasts to market without much weight loss. However, for about a century they still had to be walked from the farm to the railway, again with a corresponding weight loss. It was therefore an obvious benefit to the farmer if he could have a service that extended from the railhead to the farm. By 1932 the GWR had firmly established this kind of service, and fleet No.1550 (a Maudslay five-ton model) was one of the first vehicles with a one/two-deck livestock body.*

Above: *Another example of a vehicle used in agricultural service was this four-ton Maudslay, which is fitted with what is called a 'special empties body'. Numbered 1550 (later 4155), it states it was allocated to Lostwithiel for the purpose of returning empty milk churns to the supplying farms, but this is somewhat puzzling as it does not appear to have served there and empty churns were returned by the collecting lorries. The line drawing for this vehicle also shows a completely flat bed, and does not allow for the boxed-in wheel arches.*

Right: *Originally a 30-cwt Thornycroft, GX 3244 was allocated to the joint GWR/LMS Express Cartage Service as No. A.13. It was cascaded down and strengthened to two-tons and was given a cattle-carrying body in September 1932 and became No.2444, before being finally re-numbered 2173.*

Above: *The Thornycroft PB models in the Express Cartage Service fleet were all re-allocated to either general cartage or became non-revenue-earning vehicles between 1929 and 1932, with several being returned to the Basingstoke factory of their manufacturer in order to have them 'strengthened'. Around 100 vehicles were so treated, and here we see No.2016 (a 'four-ton pneumatic' Thornycroft) in October 1930 with drop-side body G.1521. Note the vast array of goods waiting to be delivered, including a pushbike, a roll of chain link fencing, and a somewhat battered-looking suitcase.*

Left: *Another re-build in May 1931 saw 2223 emerge as 'a six-ton Thornycroft Pneumatic' fitted with a 16-foot flat-bed with detachable sides (G.1923) to Swindon Drawing 93426.*

Above: *It was not only Express Cartage Service vehicles that were cascaded down and given a second lease of life, but so too were other members of the fleet. In the first part of the GWR story, we discussed the company's bus services at length, and whilst we have no buses in this edition, this Maudslay four-tonner actually started its life as a passenger-carrying vehicle. Rebuilt in 1933 to fleet number 1512, VY 8570 was given a 'Special Body For Churn Traffic.' Note the high staves to body G.1699, the mesh sides and the roof chains designed to keep the empties in place. This lorry later became 4154.*

Above: *The expansion of the Railhead service from 1932 onwards meant that the GWR had to provide a substantial number of new vehicles. Although they may not have been 'new' in the strictest sense of the word, even the re-conditioned chassis were given new bodies to one of four standard types. Each of these bodies were divided into four types, full box van, full-tilt van, half-tilt or flat-bed with detachable sides and hoop and tilt. This new two-ton Morris Commercial (No.2800) with the van body is seen at Swindon in September 1932.*

Left: *Also found at Swindon, but about three months later, is a refurbished one-ton Morris Commercial with the full-tilt van body. Numbered 1062, this 1920s model would not last to enter into the re-numbering scheme that the GWR later introduced.*

Top Right: *Formerly joint GWR-LNER Express Cartage Van A155, this two-ton Morris was another conversion of the 1930s. It was part of a series that began in 1937 to create Emergency Repair Units for the Signalling & Telegraph Department. This began in 1937 and the example here was finished as A4055 on 28th January 1939. The fundamental design of the Express Cartage van body called for a 'walk-thru' door to the cab and slatted hardwood floor. The back end of the vehicle was painted off-white, presumably to aid in the black-out conditions that were envisaged war would necessitate; EYV 758 was allocated to the S&T Engineer in Neath. Note that side-windows and rudimentary seating has been provided for the S&T gang members who would accompany this van.*

Below: *What a surprise this image turned out to be, for it is none other than a Guy Motors Ant 'evaluation' vehicle. This tractor was loaned to the GWR in April 1937, but had been made for military tests in Wales that summer. It carries a military pattern cab, on which very angular lines are clearly evident. This style of Specification 36A cab, devised by Guy, would later become standard on many British Army trucks and field tractors for two reasons. The first of these was the economy of manufacture, as the panels did not have to be beaten into shape, the other being the ease of cleaning, which was considered essential should chemical-gas attack take place. The Blackburn registration number (DBV 984) is something of a mystery however, as it was not officially issued until December 1950, when it was allocated to an Austin car.*

Above: *From the many comments we have had from railway modellers, we know that readers like to see different views of the same vehicle, so this pair of views showing a Fordson 7W two-tonner should fit the bill nicely! The front off-side view shows A2788 (FGT 500) with body C.2779. Although lettered, like most GWR vehicles as Paddington Station, it was in fact allocated to the Chief Mechanical Engineer at Swindon Works on 6th April 1939.*

Left: *Here we see the same vehicle, but this time from the rear near-side. This aspect is especially interesting as the flat-bed has been fitted with 'Pipe or Bar Carrying Brackets'. These enabled extra-long items to be carried down the vehicle's near-side, extending the length down the side of the cab and a leather strap (seen by the cab) was used to secure them.*

Top Right: *In the first book on this subject, we showed images of A3014 (FLL 388) and A3082 (FYU 207) and stated that the Fordson 7W was a 'relatively rare model in railway service'; oh dear, how wrong we were! As we later discovered during 1938-9, the GWR purchased no less than 200 Fordson 7W models, thanks to state-funding that was designed to help buy new vehicles that could fulfil both railway and civil defence duties. In the next picture of these 'rare' beasts, we see A3016 with body C.2795. This was ostensibly a flat-bed, but it did have fixed sides at the cab-end as this picture clearly shows. Not only would the body number be painted on to the white panel containing the word Great, from Great Western Railway, the serial number would also be burned into the woodwork. In this vehicle, the serial number can be seen twice, once at the front end and once at the back, just next to the word Railway. It was built in this guise in late-1938, but is pictured here in April 1940 having just been out-shopped by Swindon Works after being given the 'blackout-ARP' paint scheme.*

Bottom Right: *Here we have another rear near-side view of a 7W (A3014), showing a straight-forward flat-bed body on FLL 388. This is the same vehicle as featured on page 40 of Part I, but it shows much more detail. For a start, it makes an interesting comparison with the picture above, as it illustrates the difference between civilian and wartime liveries on the same kind of vehicle. When compared with A2788 opposite, it shows the difference between the Ford standard cab (on A2788) and the GWR Safety Cab (on A3014). The most significant factor is that the GWR cab is far wider, and only utilises the Fordson scuttle. It can also be seen that just one window aperture is located in the back of the cab and even that is 'blanked out'. It also shows the kerb window on the cab's near-side, so a driver could safely position his vehicle when pulling up at a kerb - something these lorries did dozens of times a day when on local delivery work.*

Above: *Yet a further variant on the Fordson 7W, A3011 this three-ton full-tilt-bodied model was used by the Chief Mechanical Engineer's Department at Caerphilly Works after it was acquired new on 6th April 1939. It carries an unusual kind of body (C.2747), which includes a short high-end section behind the cab and has a solid roof on which it would carry the tilt. This is the only one of these Fordson vehicles that we have seen provided with a radiator 'frost-jacket'.*

Left: *Fordson 7Ws continued to be purchased through the war years, but the records we have consulted do not seem to show just how many were acquired. This picture dates from 16th April 1946 when this view of A4645 was taken, but whether this was a view on acquisition or at an overhaul we cannot say.*

Left: *Interestingly, it appears that towards the end of World War II, a shortage of truck chassis saw the GWR sending vehicles out to their operating bases with two separate bodies, which would be exchanged one for the other depending on the kind of work being undertaken. For instance Slough had need of this livestock body G.3562, which was designed for use on a five-ton truck chassis. It is pictured here at Swindon Works prior to departure, mounted on to a Thornycroft vehicle that had come in for refurbishment. The background of the picture is equally interesting, as it shows the works still wearing its green and black camouflage painting, whilst horse-drawn drays and tilts are seen to the right on the Thornycroft; note the brand-new and un-bodied Scammell Mechanical Horse trailer chassis seen on the left.*

Below: *And here we have the vehicle that would be used to carry the livestock body around Berkshire. It is a Vulcan six-tonner, GYM 5 (what would that registration plate be worth today?). Careful examination of the picture will reveal how easy it would have been to lift the flat-bed platform (body G.3159) from the chassis, but one suspects that the livestock body would have been more problematical. Indeed, this is what turned out to be the case, and the 'interchangeable body' idea only lasted for about 12 to 18 months on new builds, and about two to three years on existing vehicles.*

Above: *In the first book on GWR road vehicles, we carried on page 41 bottom, a view of a Dennis Jubilant Six-Wheeler, fleet number S29012 (HGP 734), mentioning that its rear tailgate was painted cream and it had a cut-out semi-circle to allow the rear lights to show when the vehicle was travelling with its tailgate down. That picture was too poor to reproduce, but the same cannot be said of S9013 (HGP 735), which was purchased for the S&T Department in 1946.*

Right: *Before we leave the wartime era, we cannot forget to show this October 1941 view of a former Daimler limousine, which was purchased by the company and converted into a works ambulance at Swindon. Given fleet number 233, its white-tipped wings, wheel arches and hooded headlamps reflect the black-out conditions.*

Tractors & Trailers

Following the lead taken by the London, Midland & Scottish Railway, the GWR rapidly found a use for the 'Mechanical Horse', operating examples by both Karrier Motors of Huddersfield and Scammell of Watford. As we discussed these at length in our **Nostalgia Road** book, *Mechanical Horses* by Bill Aldridge, and to a lesser extent in the first book on GWR road vehicles, we will not cover that ground in detail again, save to say that the GWR did develop a fascinating fleet of trailers, with myriads of different types in use.

They also had larger tractor units as well, mostly four-wheel tractors based around the Thornycroft Nippy or Morris Commercial chassis, which in turn usually carried 'Safety Cabs' manufactured by the GWR at Swindon, Slough and Wolverhampton.

Above: *Here we have a Morris Commercial three-ton tractor with a Wolverhampton-built 'Safety Cab' (job no. W3/399, the date of which has been traced back to September 1939. As can be seen, the vehicle originally carried fleet number 4027, but this was later changed to 6227. It is paired, via a Scammell coupling, to a Taskers 'straight frame' trailer No. T1558*

Right: *In 1946, the Great Western were allocated a number of ex-War Department Leyland draw-bar tractors, such as A1046 seen here at Paddington shortly after refurbishment. Later allocated fleet number 401, UX 1400 displays its powerful back end, which is equipped with an independently-powered two-speed, heavy-duty winch. Of these Robin Jenner states, "these Leyland's were previously used in connection with anti-aircraft batteries and barrage balloon defences around London during the war".*

Top Left: *The development of the Mechanical Horse trailer would take a book to explain in its own right, and in the space available we can only scratch the surface of the subject. The two images on this page show a GWR DYAK G trailer. Fleet number T-1267, was a six-ton model built by the firm of Crane's of Dereham.*

Bottom Left: *The rear off-side view of T-1267, provides even further detail of the back axle and the Scammell coupling. The substantial tyres are Goodyear All-weather, and used to enable the trailer to carry the heavier payloads.*

By the 1920s, standardisation in both vehicle chassis and body types had become of the very utmost importance to the GWR's Road Motor Department, which had its central workshops and head office at Slough. As the process of change (from horse-haulage to motor vehicles) speeded up, standardisation became even more important, and nowhere was this needed more than in the huge fleet of mechanical horse trailers, that the company were buying. By the late-1930s, the company owned 3.7 trailers for every one of the Mechanical Horse tractor units.

The standard Mechanical Horse flat-bed trailer had of course been developed by the LMS from their standard three-ton dray. Indeed, it had the LMS's intention to convert its existing fleet of horse-drawn trailers, so that they could be pulled by the three-wheeled tractor units. The early experiments with the Karrier Cob had shown that such trailers *could* be converted by removing the front axle and shafts and substituting a mechanical coupling, but at the same time the original back-axle and wheels were too weak to give any longevity of service. All of this is detailed in our earlier railway road vehicle books and also *Mechanical Horses*, by Bill Aldridge. Those books will then show how the range of trailers rapidly expanded, so that a trailer was soon available for almost every kind of job.

Generally, the majority of the trailers would be simple flat-bed models. As can be seen from the pictures on page 30, many of the trailers had a one-plank fixed sidebar and drop-down tailgate. They were also provided with five tilt frame brackets on each of the fixed sides, and these allowed metal hoops to be fitted so that a canvas tilt could be used. Careful examination of these brackets will further reveal that the tilt could be set to two different heights. The same brackets could also be used for fitting deeper sides, either of the fixed or drop-side variety.

This ensured that the standard trailer was very versatile indeed, and modellers can make many variations on a theme. In 2005, the die-cast model manufacturer Corgi launched a six-ton Mechanical Horse in their 'Trackside' range of 4mm/1:76/OO Gauge models, and it soon became available in the livery of GWR, LMS, LNER and BR. It also came with one of three trailers, flat-bed, drop-side and box van. From the images shown here, we imagine that a variety of different trailer types could be produced by enterprising modellers using only a basic level of skills and equipment.

Top Right: *Because many of the buildings that the GWR served with their cartage fleet were built in the Victorian era (or earlier), access to them was often very narrow indeed. To provide a service to such buildings, the DYAK.NF trailer was designed. Literally meaning Narrow Frame, the three-ton flat-beds like T-1548 could gain access to buildings with the tiniest of entry-ways.*

Bottom Right: *An interesting version of the DYAK.G was this semi-covered trailer, which was originally T-1848. It has half-drop-sides, a half canvas tilt and a tarpaulin frame extending the full length of the bed. Close examination of the picture will reveal how the metal frames on the side supported both the tilt hoops and the drop-sides. Later on this kind of trailer became the DYAK.OS, and this one was re-numbered T-6949.*

Top Left: *Here we have two examples of trailers with sides, all of which are fitted with Firestone tyres. The first is a six-ton AL trailer with fixed sides, which was coded DYAK OG. It has no frame brackets for use with a canvas tilt, but it does have tie-down hooks so that the load could be roped down. It also has a drop-down tailgate, originally entering service in September 1938 as T-1780, it would later be re-numbered T-6951.*

Bottom Left: *By contrast T-1679 was a DYAK OH, which was a three-ton detachable side trailer. Once again close examination will show how the sides, headboard and tailgate were detachable to allow its use as a flat-bed trailer. The size of the headboard also varied, and the author has seen images of DYAK.OH trailers with three, four, five and even six planks. Presumably the higher the headboard, the bulkier the load; for instance a six-plank trailer picture showed it loaded with bales of cotton at Birkenhead Docks.*

The standardisation of the trailer fleet was very important to all the railway companies, especially following the two lines of development that were ongoing during the mid-1930s. The LMS had, with Karrier Motors of Huddersfield conceived the idea of replacing their horse stud with a mechanical device. Meanwhile, the LNER were experimenting with Napier and later on Scammell.

This development was actually a reaction to the Depression of the early-1930s, just as the steam locomotive had been in the troubled times of the Napoleonic War. Both events showing that, in times of adversity, keeping beasts of burden could be a costly exercise. When food-stuff was dear, as it was in the early-19th century, horses were too expensive to run - hence the need for a Mechanical Horse (steam engine) to replace them. Likewise when road traffic had a downturn, horses still had to be fed daily, so a Mechanical Horse for road haulage was also going to be a distinct advantage.

As there was going to be a massive demand for Mechanical Horses, it was decided that it was better to standardise on one coupling, so in 1934 the 'Big Four' companies got Scammell to agree to letting their coupling be used by other manufacturers under licence.

This simplified the whole cartage operation, and the GWR saw that not only was their an advantage in standardising on the tractor trailer couplings, but that the creation of standard types of trailer would be essential. Again the trailer frames would be of Scammell design, but would be made by a variety of companies. All the trailer firms were very busy, and the 'Big Four' committee dealing with standardisation allocated each railway a 'primary' trailer manufacturer in addition to Scammell, the GWR thus began with Taskers but they were soon joined by supplies from Hands and Cranes.

Top Right: *One of the GWR's maxims in the operation of its road motor fleet was versatility, and this led to certain vehicles being used for different purposes on different days of the week. This was also seen with the DYAK.K trailers, which were a half-tilt van design with fixed sides. Many of these were painted in service brown and had removable side-boards. The body would be simply painted GWR, however by the use of removal boards, the trailer could be converted to 'Country Lorry Service', 'Express Cartage' or even have a manufacturers nameboard like Cadbury etc. This DYAK K (T-1381), appears to have its Express Cartage sign firmly fixed.*

Bottom Right: *However, if T-1381 had been a regular member of the express fleet, it would have normally had its upper half body painted in cream, as seen on this full van body DYAK OC. Like T-1381 it has a large grey panel on which advertisements could be pasted, but a distinct division between the upper and lower body panels to give the impression that this vehicle was part of the passenger coach fleet. In the later re-numbering it became T4451.*

RAILHEAD SERVICES

As outlined in the first part of the GWR road vehicle story, from the end of World War I onwards, the company began to expand its road operations from selected railheads in the guise of the 'Country Lorry Service'. This was primarily intended to serve the agricultural community, delivering anything from seeds to tractors and on the return runs collecting whatever kind of produce that the farm had for sale.

A great many of the old AEC YB- and YC-Type lorries were transferred to this service although their solid wheels and open cabs can not have been all that conducive to those who had to drive them on country lanes or farm tracks. However, photographic evidence suggests most of these 'country lorries', had their perambulator style cab hoods replaced by an open-fronted wooden cab, whilst the flat-bed platforms behind were given either slatted sides or drop-sides. The AECs were not the sole custodians of this duty, as Thornycroft PB and Associated Daimler 508 models also figured largely. Cattle-truck, horse-box and mixed livestock bodies also appeared, greatly enhancing the flexibility of the Railhead Service.

With many rural stations offering the Railhead, Country Lorry and the Express Parcels services, the hinterland around them considerably opened up for the GWR and other business users were not slow to see the potential this offered to their businesses. It was quite obvious that by sending bulk supplies of their products to a railway depot, where it could be split into smaller lots, considerable savings could be made in delivery costs. This was a factor especially important to businesses supplying consumable products to the retail trade.

Left: *At Railhead Distribution Stations, the GWR provided manufacturers with road vehicles to continue the onward road journey to their customers. Some used vans specially painted in the manufacturer's colour scheme and dealt solely with their products. However many of the rural 'routes' simply did not provide for sufficient traffic to operate a van exclusively for five and a half days a week, so use was made of removable advertising boards as seen on this Thornycroft two-ton van used on the Macfarlane, Lang contract at Redruth, Cornwall in January 1926.*

Top Right: *A second view of van No.976, which would later be re-numbered 1827.*

Bottom Right: *By contrast we see here an 'exclusive' Railhead delivery vehicle, No.2575. A normal-control Morris two-ton van, it had a GWR chassis designation R13/40 and a Swindon-built body to Lot W3/307. Outshopped on 24th March 1933, it was painted in the all-over Macfarlane, Lang livery and fitted with a 10' x 2' empty biscuit tin roof rack. In the later re-numbering sachem it would become No.2237.*

With this we got the basis for what the modern world now calls logistics and mass distribution, so it is not surprising that big names in the industry of that day (like Cadbury, Rowntree and Macfarlane-Lang) would be big supporters of the GWR Railhead scheme.

The benefit of a comprehensive delivery and warehousing system was of considerable advantage to firms such as these, as was the promotional value of having delivery vehicles lettered with all-over advertising.

There was another advantage in that the drivers and warehouse staff, who dealt with the Railhead and Break-Bulk schemes, became well-versed in the products they were dealing with. Many of these identified themselves with the manufacturer, caring for their needs in a way that just did not happen with 'loose' goods.

Above: *Here we see No.979 a Burford two-ton van with a body built at the GWR's Wolverhampton Works to Lot 150. Registered YH 7477, it was allocated to Taunton for several years. Again it features a two foot deep rack for the carriage of empty biscuit tins, which in those days carried a redeemable deposit.*

Left: *Number 4008 was a Morris Commercial C-Type 25- to 30-cwt model, again finished in the overall livery of the customer and registered EYL 286. Based in Glasgow, Macfarlane, Lang later joined with Price & Co and then in 1946, they joined with two former rivals (Crawford and McVitie's) to form United Biscuits.*

Above: *Another Morris Commercial C-Type is found on ALN 466, GWR 2520, which was used by the famous York chocolate and confectionery manufacturer Joseph Rowntree. Painted dark green and liveried with gold signwriting this van would have looked extremely attractive when it was turned out of the paint shop at Caerphilly in June 1934. The van was then allocated to Cardiff's 'railhead' service. Note the roof rack ladder fixed to the rear of the van body.*

Right: *Interestingly, here we have a picture of No.2520 after it had been turned out of the body shop in Swindon on 9th June 1934. It clearly shows that the fleet number has been added, and GWR paint colour 254 applied to the body. This means that Caerphilly simply had to undertake the sign-writing before it entered service in early July.*

Above: *The GWR's association with Ford/Fordson chassis began just before World War II, and a substantial number of Dagenham-built products entered the fleet. These varied from Model 51 and 52 chassis, some of which had County Commercial Cars six-wheel chassis modifications, to Fordson 7W seven-ton trucks. A number of vans in 30-cwt range were employed, including No.4052 (EYV 751) for Rowntree work in Buckinghamshire.*

Left: *Allocated to Wiltshire (possibly Salisbury), another member of the fleet No.4054 (EVY 757), a Morris two-ton van, unusually bears both the original fleet number 4054 and the later 2762. The re-numbering therefore adds confusion to the fleet list, but we hope that this book will provide an impetus to get this matter resolved.*

Above: *Another great name in the world of confectionery was Cadbury, who were based at Bourneville in Birmingham - right in the heart of GWR territory. It was therefore logical for them to utilise the Railhead services in a big way. Certain depots seem to have been very prominent, including Exeter where No.2571 was based.*

Right: *Allocated fleet number 2521 (later 1532) this 30-cwt Morris Commercial was given what was known as a 'Cadbury' body, which was basically an adaptation of van body Lot W3/319. It is pictured here on completion at the Swindon Works on 26th April 1934. Like many of the images, the background (that would otherwise have revealed a lot of detail) was painted out on the negatives for the purpose of making the image of the van clearer.*

Above: *Two pictures of additional or replacement vans for the Exeter Depot are seen with views taken in 1937 and 1940 respectively. Although we have a pair of two-ton Morris Commercials, there are striking differences between the vehicles. The first is a semi-forward-control model No.2526 (DLT 253), which would later become No.2233. Its legal lettering bearing the name of F.R.E. Davis, General Manager, GWR Paddington.*

Left: *The second image shows a wartime livery on No.2789 (FYL 159), which was allocated to the Road Motor Department from Swindon Works on 30th April 1940. Unlike the previous Cadbury vehicles it now carries a white roof, and all the leading edges are painted white which, along with the shaded headlights, is part of the 'blackout' arrangements.*

Above: *The re-numbering scheme, which began in 1942 makes a confusing record of the GWR fleet! Rather than simply allocate new numbers to vehicles as they arrived, the RMD decided to use numbers that had previously been allocated to the Associated Daimler 508s, and then to the Thornycroft PBs. Here we see No.1945 not long after nationalisation in 1948. In an off-side front three-quarter view the new Morris with fared-in headlights and a body built by James Whiston of West Drayton.*

Right: *A full side view of the same vehicle picture before its allocation to Exeter. The number three in the roundel on the driver's door refers to its number in the Cadbury 'fleet' at Exeter, which in No.1945 numbered four vehicles, all Morris Commercial models.*

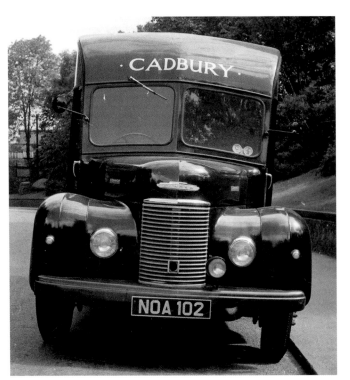

Left: *Post-war vehicle shortages and the Government's exhortation to motor manufacturers to 'Export or Die' left large fleet operators like the GWR in quite a quandary. Unable to acquire their traditionally preferred chassis, they had to take what they could get, and as a consequence a number of Commer vans entered service with the GWR in 1946. Purchases from this manufacturer continued after nationalisation, but we have no date for which NOA 102 entered the railway fleet on the Cadbury service.*

Below: *The Railhead road delivery service was of course continued by British Railways long after the GWR was nationalised at the end of 1947, but after a while the vehicles used in such service seem to have dispensed with carrying the railway fleet number. This is certainly the case with this two-ton Morris Commercial, which is fitted with a van body by Star Motor Bodies Ltd. of Warrington. Painted dark blue and white MLL 426 was photographed at Swindon Works on 26th September 1955. It would have had an internal running number in the range No.1938-9, a series that had previously been allocated to the GWR's Associated Daimler 508 vans. If anyone can help with a list of which vehicles were renumbered in this time period, the author would be deeply indebted to hear from them.*

POST-WAR ACQUISITIONS

As outlined earlier, many of the post-1945 acquisitions were allocated serial numbers of vehicles that had been scrapped. Whilst others were re-numbered and also given the fleet numbers of older vehicles, some new models were given entirely new fleet numbers, and the situation is therefore most confusing.

This Page: *One vehicle to acquire a previously un-allocated fleet number was 3698 (MLL 462) a Morris FV12/5 three-ton flat-bed with hinge-divided detachable sides. The body (G.4684) was built to Drawing No. D1218 and Lot 901. It was ordered for use by the Chief Civil Engineer's Department and spent most of its life in the Plymouth District.*

Above: *Allocated a 'new' fleet number, B 5103W (the W denotes Western Region), this Vulcan was given a one-and-a-half-deck milk churn body (G.4262). It is seen at the Road Motor Department in Slough before allocation to Herefordshire, where it would spend its days trundling the country lanes loaded with milk churns. The body was built to Drawing E1800.*

Left: *To cater for the shortfall in vehicles that the GWR were experiencing, a decision was taken in 1948 to transfer other vehicles that may be surplus on other regions. Thus, when a fleet of two-ton Dennis Triton lorries was delivered to the London Midland Region, four of them were transferred to the Western Region, where they became numbers 1900,16,18 and 24, which were fitted with flat-bed bodies G.4621-4 at Slough.*

The problem with trying to present an accurate fleet list after 1942 is certainly confused by new acquisitions being given old fleet numbers on a piecemeal basis, and the fact that fleet numbers and registration numbers did not run in consecutive order. For those people who make a study of such things, it becomes quite frustrating, and probably for this reason alone. nobody has been able to present an accurate listing of GWR vehicles. When it became part of the British Railways fleet, it become increasingly desperate.

To many readers this will not matter one jot, but for those who want to create an accurate model it can be of supreme importance. Sadly, even the commercial die-cast manufacturers tend to get it wrong as well, but we felt it was worth exploring the subject to see if we could present a logical sequence of fleet numbers in the GWR fleet at least!

Above: *One of the big problems faced by railway road vehicle fleet number recorders, is the fact that so many numbers were re-issued. Initially the fleet number 1655 was part of a batch of Guy ONB bus chassis that were registered in the UV 9*** series and placed in service with fleet numbers 1646-61. It will be recalled from the first part of this story, the GWR bus fleet was eventually taken out of full railway ownership and merged in to fleets like Western National and Western Welsh. This therefore meant that the numbers that had been allocated to these vehicles had become spare, and were suitable for re-use. As a consequence, when this Morris was acquired by the Western Region in 1958, it was allocated the number A1655 (the A standing for additional. It carries a half-tilt and van body (G.3920) that was made at Slough; the Morris was then allocated to Oakhampton in Devon.*

Fleet List

Following the earlier railway road books, we have been repeatedly asked about the possibility of publishing a fleet list, but despite extensive research we have not found anything that looks in the least accurate. The most respectable is the list of GWR buses published by the GWR Society, but the subject is fraught with problems. The biggest problem is the way in which the GWR numbered its fleet, and the way it also changed the use of vehicles from one mode of transport to another. The ex-WD Disposal Board AEC YB and YC Types are a nightmare, but so too are other members of the fleet. For example, problems with the delivery of the Durkopp vehicles saw the order being cancelled part way through, and the numbers 68-72 re-allocated to other vehicles - though precisely what we have no idea. The argument is therefore not to publish any list until you can be absolutely sure, or is it?

For the sake of debate, and not casting anything in tablets of stone, I would offer this list which was started by the late-David Cantrell, whose step-father was the Repair Shop Manager at the GWR Road Motors Department in Slough. David himself served a motor engineering apprenticeship with Citroen Cars in Slough and always kept an interest in the GWR operation.

David's record-keeping was aided by his father and step-brother, who also worked in the GWR RMD, and his data has been very useful in my research. However, to add to this baseline, we have looked extensively at all the original GWR road vehicle pictures that have come in to our possession, as the backs of these pictures contain much useful information, showing (as they often do), not just the vehicle in question, but the full details of the other vehicles in the same batch. Body drawings we have studied, often show the Lot Numbers, the fleet numbers and the registration dates of the vehicles. The bodies would also be added, but sometimes only one or the other would be used. Hence we have fleet numbers without registration numbers, and registration numbers without fleet numbers.

Despite this, GWR officials did not always get it right, and we have found drawings that say the body was allocated to say a Thornycroft Nippy, when photographic evidence shows it was fixed on a Fordson three-tonner. We even have Swindon Drawing Office photographs that say on the back the name of one chassis manufacturer, when quite clearly the image shows a different make altogether. So, please do not shoot the piano player, the list that follows is presented to the best of our information, and it seems very logical in view of the evidence we have before us, but no doubt others will know the truth!

FLEET NO.	REGISTRATION	MAKE	BODY
E5	CM 1770	GVC 5-ton	Electric truck
E11-4	DX 1985-7	Orwell	Electric Van
E2800-1		Douglas	Electric Van
S14-16		Foden 4-wheel	Steam Lorry
S17	UL 4361	Foden 6-wheel	Tractor
S18-9	UL 4362-3	Foden 6-wheel	Steam lorry
S20	UL 4364	Foden 6-wheel	Steam lorry
1-3	AF 36-8	Milnes-Daimler 20hp	Wagonette
3D	AM 274	Dennis	Fire Engine
4	AF 61*	Milnes-Daimler 20hp	Wagonette
5-7	AF 64-6*	Milnes-Daimler 20hp	Wagonette
8	AF 153*	Milnes-Daimler 20hp	Bus
9	A 5104*	Milnes-Daimler 20hp	Bus
10	A 4261*	Milnes-Daimler 20hp	Bus
11-3	AF 74-6*	Milnes-Daimler 20hp	Bus
14	AF 80*	Milnes-Daimler 20hp	Bus
15-16	AF 84-5*	Milnes-Daimler 20hp	Bus
17-26	A 6179-87*	Milnes-Daimler 20hp	Bus
27-8	AF 96-7*	Milnes-Daimler 20hp	Bus
29-33	LC 3008-12	Durkopp	Bus
29-33D	AF 157-61*	Milnes-Daimler 20hp	Bus
34-6	DA 80, 82, 81	Clarkson 20hp	Steam bus
34D	LC 315*	Milnes-Daimler 20hp	Bus
35D	LC 2107*	Milnes-Daimler 20hp	Bus
36D	LC 2537*	Milnes-Daimler 20hp	Bus
37	A 7645*	Milnes-Daimler 20hp	Lorry
38-9	AF 281, 280*	Wolseley	Bus
40-3	LC 1083-6	Wolseley 12hp	Van
40-43D	BH 01-4*	Milnes-Daimler 20hp	Van
44	CO 112*	Milnes-Daimler 20hp	Lorry
45-47	AF 86-8*	Straker-Squire	Van
48-9	DA 100	Durkopp 20hp	Bus
48D	LC 3636	Milnes-Daimler	Lorry
50	LC 1171	Durkopp	Bus
49-50D	CO 125/8*	Milnes-Daimler 20hp	Lorry
51-53	A 9733-5*	Maudslay	Bus
53D	K 1564*	Milnes-Daimler 20hp	Bus/Van
54-5	O 1774/61	Wallis & Stevens	Tractor
56-7	O 1772-3	Avelling & Porter	Tractor
56-7D	K 1565-6*	Milnes-Daimler 30hp	Bus/Van
58-61	AF 145-8*	Milnes-Daimler 30hp	Bus
62-75	?	Durkopp	Van/Bus
62D	?	Milnes-Daimler 30hp	Bus
63D	BH 014	Wolseley 20hp	Bus
64-75D	AF 188-99*	Milnes-Daimler 30hp	Bus
75-6D	AF 173-4*	Milnes-Daimler 30hp	Bus
77D	BH 015	Wolseley 33hp	Bus
78-80	AF 160-2	Straker-Squire	Bus
81-2	U 307-8	Yorkshire Steam	Wagon
82D	LC 4338	Riker Electric.	Van
83-7	AF 223-7*	Milnes-Daimler 30hp	Bus
88	AF 268	Wolseley 33hp	Bus
89-94	AF 269-70	?	?
95	BH 020	GWR Electric.	Lorry
96	LC 3523	Milnes-Daimler 30hp	Bus
97	LC 6702	Milnes-Daimler 30hp	Bus
98	LC 4415	Milnes-Daimler 30hp	Bus
99	LC 6704	Milnes-Daimler 30hp	Bus
100	LC 6706	Milnes-Daimler 30hp	Bus
101	LC 2538	Milnes-Daimler 30hp	Bus
102-4	LC 6703/0/1	Milnes-Daimler 30hp	Bus
105-8	CM 391-94	Straker-Squire	Van/Bus
109-11	O 4504-6	Straker-Squire	Van
112	T 1690	Milnes-Daimler 30hp	Bus

No.	Registration	Make	Type
113	T 1720*	Milnes-Daimler 30hp	Bus
114-5	DL 254-5*	Milnes-Daimler 20hp	Bus
116-8	AF 544/57-8*	Milnes-Daimler 30hp	Bus
119-21	LD 7190-92 *	Auto Carrier	Trike
122D	LC 3418*	Straker-Squire	Van
126-7	?	Maudslay	Bus
128	DLL 290	Austin	Car
129-140	?	Maudslay	Bus
141	AF 781	Milnes-Daimler 30hp	Bus
142D	AF 782	Straker-Squire 15-cwt	Bus/Van
143-150	BF 01-8*	Milnes-Daimler 30hp	Bus
151-2	?	Milnes-Daimler 30hp	Charabanc
153-154	AF 705/7/14	Dennis 20hp	Bus
155-62	AF 717-24	Dennis 20hp	Bus
163-5	LE 9606/25/09	Commer	Lorry
166-7	LE 9658/33	Commer	Lorry
168-9	AF 651-2*	Milnes-Daimler 30hp	Bus
170-1	AF 683-4*	Milnes-Daimler 30hp	Bus
173	K 1604	Milnes-Daimler 30hp	Van/bus
174	?	Knox	Tractor
178-80	T 3593-5	Maudslay 30hp	Bus
180D	LL 787	Adler	Car
181	K 1564*	Milnes-Daimler 30hp	Bus
184	LT 9897	AEC Y-	
191-9	T 6670-8*	AEC 45hp	Coach
193D	XK 1561	Austin	Car
194D	BO 3510	Austin	Car
195D	XL 9625	Austin	Car
196D	XL 9624	Austin	Car
197-8D	XM 1025-6	Austin	Lorry
200	?	Thornycroft	Van
201-04	T ****	Maudslay	Bus
205	HL ****	Maudslay	Bus
213-15	AB 4033-5	Maudslay	Bus
216-24	T ****	AEC YC 45hp	Coach
223D	?	Daimler	Ambulance
225-31	T ****	AEC Y/YB 45hp	Coach
232	BH 0274	AEC Y/YB 45hp	Coach
233-50	T ****	AEC Y/YB 45hp	Coach
253-5	AF 2681-3	AEC Y 45hp	Charabanc
256-8	AF 2678-80	AEC Y 45hp	Charabanc
259-60	XK 9102-3	AEC	Coach
261-2	XK 9930-1	AEC	Coach
263-6	XL 1791-4	AEC	Coach
267-8	XL 4858-9	AEC	Coach
269	XN 6318*	AEC	Coach
270-2	XN 6321/20/19*	AEC YC	Coach
273	LX 8013	AEC YC	Coach
274	LX 8182	AEC YC	Coach
275	LU 3917	AEC YC	Coach
276	LX 8263	AEC YC	Coach
277	LX 8133	AEC YC	Lorry
278	LX 8182	AEC YC	Coach
279	LU 9589	AEC YC	Lorry
280	LX 9743	AEC YC	Lorry
281	LU 9843	AEC YC	Lorry
282	XO 7577	AEC YC	Lorry
283	LX 9728	AEC YC	Lorry
284	XO 7577	AEC YC	Lorry
285	XN 2265	AEC YC	Lorry
285A	CGN 999	Austin 20hp	Ambulance
286	XM 9791	AEC	Lorry
287	CY 2646	AEC 45hp	Bus
288-90	T 8148-50	AEC YC	Lorry
291	TX 178	AEC 202	Bus
292	CY 2645	AEC 45hp	Bus
293	NY 9842	AEC 202	Bus
294	NY 1580	AEC 202	Bus
295	LY 8663	AEC	Lorry
301	LL 1561	Milnes-Daimler	Van
306-10	LL 5009-13	Milnes-Daimler	Van
311	Y 2629	Straker-Squire 1-ton	Van
323	LL 7779	Milnes-Daimler	Van
324-30	XF 50*	Ford 1-ton	Lorry
331	XK 1361	Ford	Flat-bed
340-6	?	Burford Electric	Trolley
347-356	XU 2154-63	Chevrolet LQ	Bus
365	CC2671	Daimler 40hp	Bus
366-7	CC 2672/2083	Daimler 30hp	Bus
368	CC 3914	Daimler 40hp	Bus
369	CC 2082	Daimler 30hp	Bus
370	CC 1857	Thornycroft	Bus
377	AF 7844	Lancia	Charabanc
378	AF 2370	Leyland	Bus
386	YK 3835	Fordson	Tractor
387	XY 6393	Austin 12	Car
390	?	Fordson	Tractor
391	TX 178	AEC 202	Bus?
394	XO 9128	Austin	Car
396	XO 3936	Austin	Car
398-9	XN 6324/23	Austin	Car
401	?	AEC YB	Lorry
409	LT 9968	AEC	Bus
411	LT 9967	AEC	Lorry
417	LY 9369	AEC	Bus
422	AC 94	AEC YB	Lorry
423(?)	LY 9371	AEC YC	Lorry
426-7	AC 7355-6	AEC	Charabanc
428	AC 7354	AEC	Van
429	AC 7357	AEC	Charabanc
430-8	AC 73**	AEC	Lorry
439	T 9705	AEC	Bus
440-1	T 9707/6	AEC	Van
442	T 9711	AEC	Charabanc
443	Y 7392	AEC	?
444	LY 9540	AEC YC	Lorry
445-6	FB 2705-6	AEC YB	?
447	XC 9851	AEC	Charabanc
448-9	TA 32-3	AEC YB	Lorry
450-1	TA 58-9	AEC YB	Charabanc
452	BH 7725	AEC YB	Bus
453	HT 3718	AEC	Bus
454-5	TA 35-6	AEC YB	Bus
456	BH 7870	AEC YB	Bus
457	BH 7723	AEC	Bus
458-9	BH 7868-9	AEC	Bus
460	BH 7724	AEC	Bus
461	BH 7871	AEC	Bus
462-3	XN 2260-1	AEC	Lorry
464-9	XN 22**	AEC	Lorry/Van
470	XN 2266	AEC	Coach
471	TA 34*	AEC YB	Lorry
472	XN 2267	AEC	Coach
473	XN 2264	AEC	Coach
474	XN 2269	AEC	Lorry
475	XN 2265	AEC	Coach
476	XO 7568	AEC YC	Coach
475	XO 7569	AEC YC	Lorry
476	XM 9791	AEC	Coach
477	LX 8298	AEC YC	Lorry
478	LX 8111	AEC YC	Lorry
479	LX 81**	AEC YC	Lorry
480	LX 9803	AEC YC	Lorry
481	LX 8174	AEC YC	Lorry
485-6	XO 7571/0	AEC YC	Lorry
493-4	XP 4947-8	AEC YC	Lorry
495	XP 6206	AEC YC	Lorry
486	XO 7570	AEC	Lorry
495-6	XP 6206-7	AEC YC	Lorry
497-8	XP 4949-50	AEC YC	Lorry
501	LH 9237	Thornycroft	Lorry
502	LH 9227	Thornycroft	Lorry
503	LH 9244	Thornycroft	Lorry
504-5	LH 9226/5	Thornycroft	Lorry

No.	Reg.	Make	Type
506	LH 9236	Thornycroft	Lorry
507	LH 9238	Thornycroft	Lorry
508	LH 9255	Thornycroft	Lorry
514	LH 9227	Thornycroft 30cwt	Van
521	XL 8004	Burford	Coach
522	XM 1017	Burford	Bus
523-30	XM 1018-24	Burford	Van
524A	FLL 383	Commer 15-cwt	Lorry
540	XN 5709	Burford	Van
546-56	XP 2153-63	Burford	Van
558	XP 1275	Burford	Van
563-5	XO 6585-7	Burford	Coach
566	XO 7576	Burford	Coach
567	XO 6588	Burford	Coach
568	XO 7575	Burford	Coach
569	XO 6589	Burford	Coach
570	XO 7574	Burford	Coach
571	XO 7573	Burford	Lorry
572	XO 7572	Burford	Lorry
574	XP 4953	Burford	Flat-bed
575	XP 7599	Burford	Van
576-88	XP 7600-12	Burford	Van
589-90	XP 7573-74	Burford	Van
591	XU 8496*	Burford	Coach
592-4	XT 8687-89	Burford	Van
595	XU 5706	Burford	Van
596	XU 7213	Burford	Van
597-9	XW 4659-61	Burford	Van
601	LX82**	AEC YC	Lorry
602	LX 8010	AEC YC	Lorry
603	LX 8129	AEC YC	Lorry
607	LX 8145	AEC YC	Lorry
608	LX 8130	AEC YC	Lorry
620-2	LX 8002-4	AEC YC	Lorry
623-6	LT 9936-39	AEC YC	Lorry
640-1	LT 9996-97	AEC YC	Lorry
644-5	LU 9152/58	AEC YC	Lorry
646(?)	LU 9591	AEC YC	Lorry
648	LU 9870	AEC YC	Lorry
651	LU 9876	AEC YC	Lorry
663-6	LX 8216-9	AEC YC	Lorry
667	LX 8015	AEC YC	Lorry
668	LX 8221/20	AEC YC	Lorry
670	LX 8014	AEC YC	Lorry
671	LX 8229	AEC YC	Lorry
672	LX 8232	AEC YC	Lorry
673	LX 8236	AEC YC	Lorry
674	?	AEC YC	Lorry
675-84	LX 8239-47*	AEC YC	Lorry
685	LX 9733	AEC YC	Lorry
686-8	LX 8295-7	AEC YC	Lorry
689	LX 9744	AEC YC	Lorry
690-7	LX 9745-52	AEC YC	Lorry
698	LX 7981	AEC	Bus
699	LX 8253	AEC YC	Lorry
700	LX 9807	AEC YC	Lorry
701	LY 8414	AEC YC	Lorry
702-5	?	AEC YC	Lorry
703	LX 8253	AEC YC	Lorry
704	LX 9807	AEC YC	Lorry
705	LY 8414	AEC YC	Lorry
706-12	?	AEC YC	Lorry
713	XP 4951	AEC YC	Lorry
714	XP 4952	AEC YC	Lorry
715-7	VP 7566-8	AEC YC	Lorry
718-20	?	AEC YC	Lorry
721	XP 7569	AEC YC	Lorry
722-3	XP 7585-6	AEC YC	Lorry
724-5	XP 7501-1	AEC YC	Lorry
726	XP 7587	AEC YC	Lorry
727	XP 7572	AEC YC	Lorry
728-38	XP 7588-98	AEC YC	Lorry
739-41	?	AEC YC	Lorry
743	XR 7599	AEC YC	Lorry
744-9	XR 7600-05	AEC YC	Lorry
750-1	XT 1631/30	AEC	Charabanc
752-3	XT 6391-2	AEC YC	Coach
754	XT 6390	AEC YC	Coach
755-7	XT 6393-95	AEC YC	Lorry
758	XT 8677	AEC	Bus
759-67	XT 8678-86	AEC YC	Lorry
768-77	XU 4905-14	AEC YC	Lorry
778	XW 1872	AEC YC	Lorry
779	XW 4581	AEC YC	Lorry
780	XW 4595	AEC YC	Lorry
781	XW 4596	AEC YC	Charabanc
782-3	XW 4597-98	AEC YC	Lorry
784-6	XW 1873-75	AEC YC	Lorry
787	XW 4581	AEC YC	Charabanc
788	MF 2913	AEC YC	Lorry
789	MF 3024	AEC YC	Lorry
790	MX 9283	AEC YC	Lorry
791-2	XW 4595-6	AEC YC	Lorry
796	XA 8842	AEC	Charabanc
797	XM 7420	AEC YC	Lorry
798	YM 6040	AEC YC	Lorry
799	AH 0551	AEC YC	Bus
800	XU 8496	Burford	Coach
801-5	XU 6907-11	Burford	Bus
806	XU 8497	Burford	Coach
807	XY 8496	Burford	BUS
808-9	XW 632/31	Burford	Bus
810-7	XW 1876-83	Burford	Bus
818	XW 2893	Burford	Coach
819-20	XW 4564-5	Burford	Bus
821-4	XW 4662-65	Burford	Van
825	XW 4640	Burford	Lorry
826-31	XW 9511-16	Burford	Lorry
836-43	XX 1101-8	Burford	Bus
849	XX 2349	Burford	Lorry
850-1	XX 7162-3	Burford	Bus
852-7	XY 2105-10	Burford	Bus
858-68	XY 7430-40	Burford	Coach
869	YK 2837	Burford	Coach
870-1	YK 3801-2	Burford	Charabanc
872	YK 2838	Burford	Bus
873-5	YK 3803-5	Burford	Coach
876	YK 2839	Burford	Bus
877-81	YK 3806-10	Thornycroft	Coach
882-3	YK 3811-2	Burford ND	Charabanc
884-89	YK 3813-18	Thornycroft	Coach
890-1	YK 3821-20	Burford	Lorry
892-3	YM 6447-48	Burford	Lorry
894-9	YM 6655-60	Burford	Bus
901-12	XY 2093-14	Thornycroft	Coach
913-5	XY 5374-6	Thornycroft A1	Coach
916-24	XY 7441-9	Thornycroft A1	Bus
925-40	YK 3822-34	Thornycroft A1	Bus
941	YM 3065	Thornycroft A1	Horsebox
942	YM 3067	Thornycroft A1	Lorry
943	YM 3066(?)	Thornycroft A1	Bus
944	YM 3068	Thornycroft A1	Lorry
945	YM 9303	Thornycroft A1	Bus
946	YN 5671	Thornycroft A1	Lorry
947-9	YM 3069-71	Thornycroft A1	Lorry
950-1	YN 231-2	Thornycroft A1	Lorry
952-4	YM 9304-6	Thornycroft A1	Lorry
955	YN 233	Thornycroft A1	Lorry
956	YM 6449	Thornycroft A1	Lorry
957	YM 9307	Thornycroft A1	Lorry
958	YN 234	Thornycroft A1	Lorry
959	YM 9308	Thornycroft A1	Lorry
960	YM 6450	Thornycroft A1	Lorry
961	YN 5672	Thornycroft A1	Lorry

48

No.	Reg.	Make	Type
962-6	?	Thornycroft A1	Lorry
967-71	YP 1127-31	Thornycroft A1	Lorry
9672-5	?	Thornycroft A1	Lorry
976	YE 59**	Thornycroft A1	Van
978	?	Thornycroft A1	Lorry
979	YH 7477	Thornycroft A1	Van
980	YU 518	Thornycroft A1	Van
981-2	?	Burford	Van
982-3	YN 2350-51	Burford	Van
1001-4	YN 235-8	Burford	Coach
1005	YM 9309*	Burford	Bus
1008	YM 9310*	Burford	Bus
1009-11	YN 239-41	Burford	Bus
1016	?	Ford A	Van
1019	?	Morris	Van
1022	?	Ford A	Van
1024(?)	YR 2659	Ford	Tractor
1030	MO 6893	Ford	Hackney
1031	XV 7566	Thornycroft PB 6w	Lorry
1037	AF 4747	Ford	Van
1038-9	RL 5818/7159	Albion	Bus
1040	AF 1558	Studebaker	Hackney
1041	FK 3196	Overland BMT	Bus
1042	BX 6226	Graham Dodge A	Bus
1043	BX 6585	Graham Dodge A	Bus
1044	BX 6402	International SL	Bus
1045	UO 2944	Leyland PLSC1	Bus
1046	UO 5995	Leyland PLSC1	Bus
1047	UO 7160	Leyland PLSC1	Bus
1048	UO 7430	Leyland PLSC1	Bus
1050-2	XV 9411-13	Austin STC	Car
1060-1	?	Scammell	Tractor
1062	?	Morris Commercial	Tilt
1063	RF 4964	Leyland PLSC1	Bus
1064	EH 5254	Guy BA	Bus
1067	TX 2023(?)	McCormick	Tractor
1073	TX 2024	Latil B	Bus?
1074	YB 8279	Overland BMT	Bus
1077-9	GC 9683-5	Thornycroft 6w	Lorry
1080-2	UV 683-5	Scammell 10-ton	Tractor
1086	UX 1406	Leyland	Tractor
1089	UW 2593	Austin	Car
1089	?	Austin	Car
1090	?	Austin	Car
1091-2	TT 16-7	Vandys SPA	Charabanc
1093	TT 603	Vandys SPA	Charabanc
1094	T 7732	Crossley	Hackney
1095	TA 5791	Lancia	Charabanc
1096-7	TT 2188-9	Lancia	Charabanc
1098	TT 2873	Lancia	Charabanc
1098A	?	Commer	Van
1099	TT 4958	Vauxhall	Hackney
1100	AH 51*	AEC YC	Van
1101	AH 690*	Morris Commercial	Bus
1102	AH 501	AEC YC	Lorry
1103	AH 511	AEC YC	Van
1100-3A	YW 5364-7	Morris Z2	Bus
1106	?	Morris Commercial	Van
1111	LT 4267	Clement-Talbot	Bus
1112	RL 6278	Albion	Bus
1113	EP 3627	Shelvoke & Drewry	Lorry
1114	YX 1528	AEC 426	Bus
1115	YX 3055	Morris 6-wheel	Coach
1116-9	UK 5812-5	Guy FBB	Bus
1122	YX 5026	Morris 1-ton	Van
1130	YX 7026	Morris 1-ton	Van
1135	YX 52--	Lancia	Bus
1143	AX 9563	Lancia	Bus
1144	UH 1475	Lancia	Bus
1145	UH 1329	Lancia	Bus
1146	AX 9900	Lancia	Bus
1147	AX 9268	Thornycroft	Bus
1148	WO 848	Thornycroft	Bus
1150-4	YM 6650-54	Fordson	Tractor
1173	YH 5008	Austin	Car
1174	YH 9262	Austin	Car
1175	YH 7904	Austin	Car
1176	YT 1982	Austin	Car
1177	YT 3536	Austin	Car
1182	YU 5253	Fordson	Tractor
1189-4	YU 5260-5	Fordson	Tractor
1196	YU 5825	Austin	Car
1197	YX 3843	Morris Cowley	Car
1198	XV 7565	Austin	Car
1199	XV 9410	Austin	Car
1201	YR 1152	Maudslay ML3	Coach
1202	YR 1089	Maudslay ML3	Coach
1203	YR 6214	Maudslay ML3	Bus
1204	YR 1154	Maudslay ML3	Bus
1205-6	YR 6215-6	Maudslay ML3	Bus
1207-4	YR 1153/5	Maudslay ML3	Bus
1209-10	YR 6217-8	Maudslay ML3	Bus
1211-2	YR 6411-2	Maudslay ML3	Bus
1213	YR 2663	Maudslay ML3	Bus
1214-8	YR 6413-7	Maudslay ML3	Bus
1219-27	YH 3791-9	Maudslay ML3	Bus
1228-9	YU 4108-9*	Maudslay ML3B	Charabanc
1230	YU 4107*	Maudslay ML3	Bus
1231	UC 4238	Maudslay ML3	Bus
1232	YU 4106	Maudslay ML3B	Bus
1233	UC 4239	Maudslay ML3	Bus
1234-5	UC 4862-3	Maudslay ML3	Bus
1236	UC 7505	Maudslay ML3	Bus
1237-8	UC 4864-5	Maudslay ML3	Bus
1239-41	UC 7506-8	Maudslay ML3	Bus
1243-6	YH 6815-9	Guy	Bus
1247-9	YH 1943-5	Guy	Bus
1251-2	YE 7049-50	Guy	Bus
1253-7	YE 7308-12	Guy	Bus
1258-61	YE 9026-9	Guy	Bus
1262-4	YF 3916-8	Guy	Coach
1265-8	YF 711-4	Guy	Coach
1269-70	YF 6815-6	Guy	Coach
1271	YF 8222	Guy	Coach
1272	YF 8295	Guy	Coach
1273	YF 8223	Guy FBB	Coach
1274	YF 8296	Guy FBB	Coach
1275-7	YF 9506-8	Guy FBB	Coach
1278-9	YR 5746-7	Guy	Bus
1280-1	YR 715-6	Guy	Coach
1282	YF 5744	Guy	Bus
1283-5	YF 3919-21	Guy	Coach
1286	YR 5745	Guy	Coach
1287	YF 6817	Guy FBB	Coach
1288-9	YF 1941-2	Guy FBB	Coach
1290	YR 5748	Guy	Bus
1291-6	YH 1935-40	Guy	Bus
1297-9	YW 5110-2	Thornycroft A6	Coach
1300	YH 1940	Guy	Bus
1301-6	YR 6394-99	Thornycroft PB	Lorry
1307	YR 6700	Thornycroft PB	Lorry
1308-12	YR 9181-85	Thornycroft PB	Lorry
1323	YE 5049	Thornycroft PB	Lorry
1334	?	Thornycroft PB	Lorry
1336	YE 5042	Thornycroft PB	Lorry
1340	YE 5401	Thornycroft PB	Lorry
1343	YE 5406?	Thornycroft PB	Lorry
1345-49	?	Thornycroft PB	Lorry
1350	YV 5431	Maudslay	Lorry
1361	YV 1122	Thornycroft PB	Flat-bed
1363-4	YV 1123-24	Thornycroft PB	?
1382-4	YW 5027-29	Thornycroft PB	Lorry
1383	J 4442	Thornycroft PB	Lorry
1384	YW 5028	Thornycroft 4-ton	Lorry

1405-13	?	Morris	Bus
1414-15	GK 6018-9	Morris	Van
1425	GK 6031	Thornycroft PB	Van
1432-4	GK 6062-4	?	Van
1440	YW 5373	Thornycroft 5-ton	Lorry
1445	YX 5013	Thornycroft 30cwt	Flat-bed
1459	GC 9039	Thornycroft 30cwt	Lorry
1460	UC 5510	Thornycroft A1	Bus
1461-2	YV 1125-6	Thornycroft A1	Coach
1463	YW 822	Thornycroft A1	Coach
1464-5	YW 5970-1	Thornycroft A1	Coach
1466-7	YX 1529-30	Thornycroft A1	Coach
1468-70	YX 5680-2	Thornycroft A1	Coach
1471-6	XV 5107-12	Thornycroft A1	Bus
1477-9	UL 4052-4	Thornycroft A1	Bus
1480-1	GU 2933-4	Thornycroft A2	Bus
1482-7	GU 9526-31	Thornycroft A2	Bus
1488-91	UU 970-3	Thornycroft A2	Bus
1492	UV 7444	Thornycroft A1	Bus
1493	GJ 2372	Thornycroft A1	Lorry
1494	GU 2934	Thornycroft A1	Bus
1500	?	Thornycroft A1	Van
1501	UL 9486	Gilford	Coach
1502-6	YV 1102-6	Maudslay ML3	Coach
1507-12	YV 8565-70	Maudslay ML3	Lorry
1513-8	YV1107-12	Maudslay ML3	Coach
1519-23	YW 3350-4	Maudslay ML3	Coach
1524-9	YV 8571-6*	Maudslay ML3	Coach
1530	YU 4107	Maudslay ML3B	Bus
1531	YV 1113	Maudslay ML3B	Bus
1532-7	UC 9099-104	Maudslay ML3	Bus
1538	YR 1114	Maudslay ML3	Coach
1539	YV 7194	Maudslay ML3	Coach
1540-2	YR 1115-7	Maudslay ML3	Coach
1543	YV 7195	Maudslay ML3	Coach
1544	YR1118	Maudslay ML3	Coach
1545-6	YV 7196-7	Maudslay ML3	Coach
1548-9	YV 7198-9	Maudslay ML3	Coach
1550-3	YV 5431-4	Maudslay	Cattle Car
1554-9	YV 8571-6	Maudslay ML3	Coach
1560-4	YV 5430-4	Maudslay ML3	Bus
1566-70	GU 2927-32	Maudslay ML3B	Bus
1571	GU 2933	Maudslay ML3B	Bus
1572-82	UU 3012-22	Maudslay ML3B	Coach
1583-95	UU 4810-22	Maudslay ML3B	Coach
1596-9	?	Chevrolet LQ	Coach
1600	XV 9409	Guy	Coach
1601-4	ULE 9486-9	Chevrolet(?)	Coach
1605-7	UV 4079-81	Thornycroft BC	Van
1608-15	UV 4082-9	Thornycroft BC	Bus
1616-9	UV 4090-3	Thornycroft BC	Van
1620-5	GU 6353-7	Maudslay ML3B	Bus
1626-31	UU 1166-71	Maudslay ML3B	Bus
1632-6	?	Chevrolet LQ	Coach
1637A	CLR 875	Trojan	Van
1638-41	?	Chevrolet LQ	Coach
1642-4	KV 1524-6	British Chevrolet	Lorry
1645-6	KV 1527-8	Bedford	Horsebox
1647	?	Guy	Sweeper
1648-9	UV 9123-4	Guy OND	Bus
1650-1	UU 974-5	Guy	Bus
1652-3	UU 9607-8	Guy	Bus
1654-6	UV 9120-2	Guy OND	Bus
1657	UV 9413	Guy OND	Bus
1658	UV 9123	Guy OND	Bus
1659-61	UV 9414-6	Guy OND	Bus
1662-7	UU 5009-14	Morris R	Bus
1670-1	GJ 360-1	Austin	Car
1694-9	UW 4694-9	Morris Cowley	Car
1700-15	XV 5520-35	Thornycroft	Lorry/Van
1716	W 9830	Thornycroft 30cwt	Lorry
1717-51	?	Thornycroft	Lorry/Van
1792-9	?	Thornycroft	Lorry/Van
1815-99	UL 936--1040	Thornycroft 30cwt	Lorry
1816	JUV 446	Austin	Drop-side
1827A	YE 59**	Thornycroft PB	Van
1857		Thornycroft 30cwt	Flat-bed
1900-10	GU 9309-18	Associated Daimler	Lorry/Van
1911	GT 4218	Karrier Cob	Mechanical Horse
1912-9	?	Associated Daimler	Lorry/Van
1920-21	?	Associated Daimler	Tipper
1922-3	UU 5001-02	Associated Daimler	Lorry
1924-7	?	Associated Daimler	Van
1928	UL 9494	Associated Daimler	Lorry
1929-34	?	Associated Daimler	Lorry
1935-8	UL 9800-4	Associated Daimler	Lorry
1939-93	?	Associated Daimler	Lorry/Van
1945R	MLL 364	Morris Commercial	Van
1992-3	GF 9522-3	Associated Daimler	Lorry
1994-5	?	AEC Mammoth	Tractor
2000-010	GC 91**	Thornycroft	?
2011-79	GC 9156-7	Thornycroft	Van
2013	GC 9158	Thornycroft	Lorry
2014	GC 9159	Thornycroft	Van
2015-079	GC 9160-215	Thornycroft	?
2080	GU 9318	Associated Daimler	Van
2080D	UL 9846	Thornycroft 30cwt	Lorry
2081-099	?	Thornycroft	?
2100-05	?	Thornycroft	?
2106	GC 9667	Thornycroft PB	Lorry
2100-73	GX 3200-73	Thornycroft	?
2200-18	?	Thornycroft	?
2219	ALN 390	Thornycroft 2-ton	?
2220-6	GK 6120-26	Thornycroft	Van
2227	GK 6127	Thornycroft JJ	Cattle
2228-46	?	Thornycroft	
2233A	DLT 253	Morris Commercial	Van
2245A	GX 2923	Morris Commercial	Van
2247-9	GK 6147-9	Thornycroft 7-ton	Tipper
2255	GX 3335	Thornycroft JJ	Tipper
2256-66	?	Thornycroft	?
2257A	?	Morris Commercial	Van
2267	GX 3347	Thornycroft PB	Flatbed
2200-68	?	Thornycroft	?
2285	?	Thornycroft Taurus	Van
2300-5	?	Thornycroft	?
2306	?	Rushton	Tractor
2307-11	?	Thornycroft	?
2312-6	GK 6196-200	Fordson	Tractor
2330	GJ 2315	Dennis 2-ton	Van
2339	GK 6161	Dennis 30-cwt	Van
2341	** 7904	Dennis 4-ton	Lorry
2350	GJ 2317	Guy 2-ton	Van
2351-2	?	Thornycroft	?
2353-4	?	Ford A	Flatbed
2351-70	?	Thornycroft	?
2361-5A	GX 3314-8	Morris Commercial	Van
2371	?	Morris	Van
2372-98	?	Thornycroft	P
2399	BLK 359	Morris 2-ton	Van
2400-29	BLR 917-46	Thornycroft	?
2430	GX 3231	Thornycroft 2-ton	Flatbed
2431-4	GX 3202-05	Morris	?
2458-61	GX 3258-61	Associated Daimler	Van
2431-4	GX 3202-5	Morris	
2440-74	GX 3240-74	Thornycroft	Cattle
2475-7	GX 3275-7	Thornycroft	Lorry
2478	GX 3278	Thornycroft	Cattle
2500-15	GJ 2319-34	Morris 25-cwt	?
2516	?	Morris Commercial	?
2517-8	ALN 463-64	Morris 25-cwt	Van
2519	ALN 465	Morris Commercial	?
2520	ALN 466	Morris 2-ton	Van
2521	ALN 467	Morris Commercial	Van

Fleet No.	Registration	Make	Body Type
2522	CYP 386	Morris 2-ton	Van
2523-29	DLT 250-6	Morris Commercial	Van
2530	CYP 397	Morris 2-ton	Tractor
2531-7	?	Morris Commercial	Cattle
2538	BYF 284	Morris 2-ton	Tractor
2539-73	?	Morris Commercial	?
2574	?	Morris 2-ton	Van
2575-98	GX 3275-309	Morris Commercial	?
2601-39	?	Thornycroft Handy	?
2640	CLM 785	Thornycroft Handy	Lorry
2657	CLR 888	Thornycroft 2-ton	?
2700-2	GT 4217-9	Karrier Cob	Mechanical Horse
2703-10	GO 9138-45	Ford B	Tipper
2714	GX 3374	Karrier Cob	Mechanical Horse
2715-7	?	Morris 2-ton	Van
2721	DLF 648	Morris 2-ton	?
2725	GX 3835	Karrier Cob	Mechanical Horse
2735-7	ALN 365-7	Scammell 6-ton	Mechanical Horse
2741-50	?	Scammell 3-ton	Mechanical Horse
2754A	ELH 487	Dennis 2-ton	Van
2760	FLL 383	Commer 15cwt	Lorry
2761-5A	EYV 756-4	Ford Model 52	Van
2762A	EYV 757	Morris 2-ton	Van
2763-5A	EYV 756-4	Ford Model 52	Van
2767-8	EYV 756-58	Morris 2-ton	Lorry
2770-2	FGT 474-6	Thornycroft Nippy	Lorry
2773-87	FGT 477-92	Thornycroft 3-ton	?
2788	FGT 500	Fordson 2-ton	Lorry
2789	FYL 158	Morris	Van
2788-99	FGT 502-12	Fordson 2-ton	Lorry
2800-9	GX 3310-9	Morris	Van
2813	GXY 181	Karrier Bantam	Van
2815-29	ALN 358-73	Fordson B	Drop-side
2838	CYP 393	Morris 2-ton	Cattle
2839	?	Morris	Van
2870	CLC 610	Morris 2-ton	Van
2901-5	GX 3301-5	Morris 6-ton	Lorry
2936	DLX 143	Thornycroft Handy	Half-cab
2937-9	DLX 144-6	Thornycroft Trusty	Drop-side
3002	CYP 371	Scammell 3t	Mechanical Horse
3003-8	?	Fordson 7W	Cattle
3009	ALN 409	Thornycroft Handy	Lorry
3010-12	FGT 467-70	Fordson 3-ton	Lorry
3014	FLL 388	Fordson 7-ton	Van
3015-6	FYL 164-5	Fordson 3-ton	Lorry
3017-20	ALN 417-20	Thornycroft	Lorry
3021-9	?	Fordson 7-ton	Livestock
3030-41	FYL 179-90	Fordson 3-ton	Lorry
3036A	ALN 393	Thornycroft Handy	Lorry
3042-8	FYU 71-7	Fordson 3-ton	Lorry
3052-68	FYU 178-82	Fordson 3-ton	Lorry
3069	FYU 195	Fordson 7-ton	?
3077	FYU 203	Fordson 3-ton	Lorry
3082	FYU 207	Fordson 7-ton	Van
3098	JWL 686	Fordson 3-ton	Tipper
3101	CGN 997	Ford 51	6w Tipper
3105	ALN 305	Fordson 2-ton	Van
3174	BGP 236	Fordson 2-ton	Lorry
3180	GYH 74	Thornycroft Nippy	Flat-bed
3185	CUV 759	Ford 52	Livestock
3186-203	?	Fordson	?
3205	GYH 35	Thornycroft Nippy	Van
3231	CLR 895	Thornycroft Trusty	Lorry
3251-60	GX 3251-60	Thornycroft Nippy	Drop-side
3338	CGF 235	Fordson	Tractor
3339	HLY 775	Thornycroft Nippy	Drop-side
3346	HLY 782	Thornycroft Nippy	Drop-side
3406	BLB 506	AEC Monarch	Lorry
3461	CGK 921	Scammel 3-ton	Fire Engine
3509	CUV 753	?	Cattle
3510-39	?	Fordson	?
3540-9	DLF 612-23	Scammell 3-ton	Mechanical Horse
3550-99	?	Fordson	Various
36xx	Series allocated to	Scammell	Mechanical Horse
3607	BGX 977	Scammell 3-ton	Mechanical Horse
3621	BLD 502	Scammell 3-ton	Mechanical Horse
3693	BXL 912	Scammell 3-ton	Mechanical Horse
37xx	Series allocated to	Scammell	Mechanical Horse
3718	GYH 62	Scammell 3-ton	Mechanical Horse
3800-5	HGC 72-6	Karrier Bantam	Tractor
3835	HLY 921	Morris 2-ton	Van
3839A	DLT 222	Morris 2-ton	Lorry
3864	ELH 485	Morris 2-ton	Tilt
3866	ELH 387	Morris 2-ton	Van
3873	JXA 486	Scammell 6-ton	Mechanical Horse
3900	CUV 711	Scammell 6-ton	Mechanical Horse
3966-8	MLL 461/60/62	Morris Commercial	Lorry
4003	?	Morris Leader	Lorry
4007-8	EYL 825-6	Morris 30-cwt	Van
4020-7	?	Morris	Tractor
4052	EYV 751	Fordson	Van
4054	EYV 757	Fordson	Van
4055	EYV 758	Morris 2-ton	S&T Van
4104	DLT 227	Karrier Cob	Mechanical Horse
4148	DLX 136	Karrier Cob	Mechanical Horse
4200-87	?	Fordson	?
4401	?	Austin 2-ton	Van
4600	EGT 297	Scammell 30-cwt	Rigid float
4601	ELH 502	Scammell 30-cwt	Rigid float
4623	EYV 771	Fordson Sussex	Tipper
4645	GLA 200	Thornycroft Sturdy	Tractor
5008	GXD 83	Thornycroft Sturdy	Lorry
5009-12	XV 5107-12	Thornycroft A1	Bus
5052-63	GYM 1-10	Vulcan 6-ton	Lorry
5064-73	HLY 656-665	Vulcan 6-ton	Lorry
5100-19	HLY 680-99	Vulcan 6-ton	Lorry
5201-25	LLX 21-45	Dennis Pax	Lorry
6271-10	FLL 362-71	Scammell 6-ton	Mechanical Horse
6285-7	FYL 152-4	Scammell 6-ton	Mechanical Horse
6289	FYU 11	Scammell 6-ton	Mechanical Horse
6318	FYU 40	Scammell 6-ton	Mechanical Horse
6369-71	GLA 139-41	Scammell 6-ton	Mechanical Horse
8049A	GK 6149	Thornycroft	Tipper
8179	?	Bedford 2-ton	?
8150	?	Scammell 3-ton	Mechanical Horse
8180	?	Bedford OSS	Tractor
8310-5	?	Bedford OSS	Tractor
8360	KXU 471	Bedford OSS	Tractor
8525	HGP 755	Morris Commercial	Tractor
8637	JXA 311	Thornycroft Nippy	Tractor
8801-5	FLL 371-5	Thornycroft Nippy	Tractor
8806-10	?	Bedford OL	Lorry
8811-2	FLL 381-82	Bedford OSS	Tractor
8819	FYU 134	Thornycroft	Tractor
8820-5	HGP 750-5	Thornycroft Nippy	Tractor
8852	FYU 167	Thornycroft Nippy	Tractor
8800	FLL 369	Thornycroft Nippy	Tractor
8883	GXD 3	Bedford 6-ton	Tractor
8890-900	GXD 10-20	Bedford OY	Tractor
8940	KXU 546	Bedford OSS	Tractor
8913	GYE 221	Bedford 6-ton	Tractor
8934	?	Bedford OSS	Tractor
9010-6	HGP 731-8	Dennis Jubilant	drop-side
S230-9	KXU 225-334	Bedford OB	Coach
S401-2	UX 1400-1	Leyland	Tractor
S403-8	?	Leyland	Tractor
S410-29	?	Leyland	Tractor
S419D	FGT 471	Latil	Tractor
S480-2	HUL 216-8	Foden DG	Tractor

A = Additionally allocated number,
D = Duplicate vehicle,
* = Vehicle carried more than one registration no.

Please note, the body type applies to the first known use of the vehicle chassis. However, frequent re-bodying took place, especially as buses were turned into delivery vans or delivery vans became lorries as they became older.

ACKNOWLEDGEMENTS

This book would not have been possible without the assistance of a great many people, notably Peter Cantrell, the son of the late-David Cantrell, who freely made his father's notes available to me. Next I must thank Bill Gable, and his wife Ann, for travelling all the way from Reading to Appleby, to carefully convey all the pictures used to illustrate the book, and also to Gerald and Gladys Burton who accompanied them.

Thanks are also due to David Hayward for sending me his copy of a GWR fleet list, which largely confirmed the records of David Cantrell, and also the PSV Circle for their notes on the GWR bus fleet. Finally, can I say thanks to my own team comprised of my wife Larraine, son-in-law Matthew Richardson, and my daughters Bryony and Louise for all their help in producing this book.

Above: *Originally No.1816 in the GWR fleet, was a 15-cwt Thornycroft van, but when the post-war re-building was underway, the number A1816 was allocated to JUV 446, a smart little Austin truck that in turn was given drop-side body G.4005. It was allocated to the S&T Department, and is believed to have been stationed in the Birmingham area.*

Thanks must also go to Robert Berry, David Hayward and David Townend for checking the manuscript. It would also be remiss of me not to thank the dozens of individuals who have written in with small amounts of information on the GWR fleet, which in turn have often been like little pieces of a jigsaw puzzle and made the whole picture become much clearer as a result. And finally, thanks to you, the reader for supporting this publication, and thereby helping to support our endeavours to make information on this Famous Fleet so widely available.